LEADERSHIP

Finding Your Biblical Style

FRANK DUPRÉE

ISBN-13:978-1534985407

ISBN-10:1534985409

INTRODUCTION

If you are called of God to lead people then this book will bless and benefit both you and those whom you are called to lead. It is both theologically and practically sound. By the time you finish reading this book you should be able to see your leadership style clearly and you will have had the opportunity to write out both a Vision and a Mission Statement.
The first part of this book is Theological. We will look at the Leader whom the Bible calls "The Set Man". And, I think that as you go through this section you will begin to relate to the words of the Centurion who said he was "a man under authority" Matthew 8:5-13

The second part is the Practical aspect. I will deal with things like:

Relationships Discipleship Teamwork

And then lastly you will be able to see where you are concerning Leadership in the Church and what to do if you are called but not yet actively leading. It will benefit you if, as you go through this book, you keep asking yourself these two questions

What do I Love? What do I Hate?

Apostle Kelly taught me that what you love and what you hate reveals what you are passionate about. It has been said that "effective ministries grow out of passion" and Leadership has been described as "passion in action".

So whether you are leading now or will be in the future I hope that you will benefit from the 40 years of experience that have helped me come to the conclusions I am sharing with you here.

In Him,

Frank Duprée

DEDICATION

This book is dedicated to the man I believe is one of the greatest leaders in the Body of Christ today… my Spiritual Father, Apostle John P. Kelly. I have been privileged to have spent personal time with him and I have learned so much from him. He is a Patriarch in the Church who has given his life to "washing the feet" of his Sons and Daughters and leading them into their own destinies.

I also want to dedicate this book to the unsung heroes who are not looking to enlarge their tent at the expense of others but who are content to know that it is more blessed to give than to receive. Those Leaders deserve all the respect we can give them.

FOREWARD

Since I started serving in the capacity of leader more than three decades ago I have read many books related to leadership and management. Invariably, some books dealt more with leadership style, some management, some dealing with various levels and steps to leadership, and some having to do with how to recognize the kind and quality of leader a person is. Many of these books were written for a secular audience even though they all had inherent biblical principles. Furthermore, I have studied Christian Leadership both from within the Holy Scriptures as well as from extra biblical books.

When I picked up this book I was pleasantly surprised how broad and deep this book is. Broad because the author has evidently read dozens of books on leadership and has gleaned from the best of them and given the reader an impressive overview of the best of them. Deep because it is evident that the author is a reflective leader/practitioner who has many great insights to share.

Furthermore, it is also evident that the author has had years of experience studying the scriptures which he disseminates with great balance and wit. Especially refreshing for me is the fact that he accurately presents the biblical leadership methodologies reflective of the first century apostolic church - which was built upon almost two thousand years of Jewish history. All of us would do well to build our churches and ministries according to this model.

So, in summary, if you want to read just one leadership book this year that both challenges and encourages you- this is the book! If you want to learn how to build effective church leadership this book is for you. If you want to understand yourself in the context of leadership - if you want to know some of pitfalls and pratfalls of leadership- if you want to know what level of leader you are - your leadership style - and how to develop even more in leadership capacity- this book is for you!

Last but not least - I also happen to have a very close friendship and working partnership with the author for more than two decades. During that time I have seen Frank walk the teachings of this book out with integrity, intensity and perseverance. After I read the first manuscript I was thinking that I could not wait to purchase copies to give to all our emerging and functional church leaders It is like reading twenty five books condensed into one. May God use this book to bless and nurture thousands of leaders for His kingdom.

Joseph Mattera
Founder/Pastor
Resurrection Church, NYC

ENDORSEMENTS

If you are in a leadership position, or believe you are called to that place, this is a must read" book for you. Bishop Frank has his call to teach stretched to its limits in this "line by line", biblical approach to successful leadership. This is not a book to be placed on a shelf after reading but should be kept within easy reach of anyone facing the varied challenges of leadership.

Apostle Frank C. Dupree
Founding Pastor
Living Water Church, Riverhead, NY

This writing represents a clear, accurate and practical structure for credible Christian leadership in the 21st Century and beyond.

Dr. Aubrey Gregory
Newark Gospel Tabernacle

Leadership is such an important subject of discussion especially in this time when there is a shortage of competent leadership. This book written by Bishop Frank Dupree gives great insight into this subject. I have learned some of the greatest principles of leadership from him as my mentor. I am excited that he has decided to share with you some of the great lessons I have been fortunate and blessed to learn up close and personal.

Bishop Nathan J. Culver
Liberty International Ministries
Atlanta, GA

CONTENTS

Chapter One

The Set Man

The people who were a part of the Church at Jerusalem in the 1st Century knew their leaders well. They were the Men of God who first had walked with Jesus as His Disciples and then as His Apostles. Their position was given to them by The Lord and they carried on the work of the Lord. As the Church expanded more Leaders were needed to meet the demands of the ever growing Church and the Apostles trained and ordained people to lead the Church along with them. By the time we see the Apostle Paul traveling with an Apostolic Team we can see the order of the Church has been well established. They built on the foundation of the Apostles and Prophets through the wisdom given to them by The Holy Spirit and by their reading of the Sacred Scriptures which we know as The Old Testament.

Paul began to write profusely as he traveled addressing the needs of the people and also laying down guidelines for Ministry and Church expansion. We can see from the record of Scripture and the writings of the early Church Fathers that there was a very well established system developed in the Church concerning Leadership. There were the Apostles, Prophets, Evangelists, Pastors and the Teachers (see Ephesians 4:11) and Elders and Deacons/Deaconesses. Everyone knew what to do in their particular area of ministry because they had been taught and trained so well.

The Man of God who was the main Leader in the Early Church was viewed as "The Set Man". We will look at several Old Testament Scriptures as well as some in the New Testament to establish our understanding of the Set Man and his role as the main Leader of each Local Church. To understand the Ministry of The Set Man we need to see several truths and the first one is:

The "Set Man" is to be "GOD-WARD"

EXODUS 18:19-21 "Hearken now unto my voice, I will give thee counsel, and God shall be with thee: be thou for the people to **GOD-WARD**..."

This terminology was used by Moses' father-in-law Jethro when he gave advice to Moses concerning his Leadership position in Israel.

The deepest sense of the word "God-ward" is to be concerned with the things of God and Minister **TO HIM** first. When we look at this principle in the Scripture we see that the Apostles still practiced it.

In **ACTS 6** we see that there was trouble with the distribution of food, etc. in the Church. When this was brought to the attention of the Apostles, Peter rose up and said "It is not right for us (the Apostles) to leave the Word of God and serve tables". We see in the next few verses that he was talking about their time in the Word of God and Prayer. He gave a practical explanation of what Jethro called being

"**GOD-WARD**". They were to make the most use of their time by spending time reading the Word of God, Praying, Preaching and Teaching. He told them that they should choose people that they could trust to take care of these other things.

So, Peter was saying that to be God-ward means that the Minister must not be overloaded with the normal, everyday operation of the Church. They **MUST** stay focused on the things of God by studying the Word and by staying in Prayer so they might preach and teach effectively. Moses was an example of a "**SET MAN**". Titus is a good example in the New Testament. The person we call "the Pastor" is supposed to fill the role of the Set Man in a Local Congregation.

"God has Set some in the Church"

We see the Set Man very clearly in both the Old and the New Testaments:

NUMBERS 27:16,17 "Let the LORD, the God of the spirits of all flesh, **SET A MAN** over the congregation, which may go out before them, and which may go in before them, and which may lead them out, and which may bring them in; that the congregation of the LORD be not as sheep which have no shepherd."

1 CORINTHIANS 12:28 "And **GOD HATH SET** some in the church, ***first apostles***, secondarily prophets, thirdly teachers, after that miracles, then gifts of healings, helps, administrations, diversities of tongues."

In both the Old and New Testaments we see that God desires to "set" someone over His people to lead them in His ways and that the person who is "set" over the Congregation should have a "shepherds heart".

Although we commonly call the **SET MAN "PASTOR"** he or she may be any one of the Fivefold Ascension Gift Ministries of Apostle, Prophet, Evangelist, Pastor, or Teacher.

If we look at the Set Man as the type of leader Peter spoke of in Acts chapter 6 then we can clearly see that the Set Man should have the Gift Ministry of the Apostle having the full revelation of how the Church is to grow and serve both God and man. That is why the Set Man must remain Godward to receive the revelation and vision he needs to lead the flock of God. The secondary aspect of the Set Man is that he must train, equip and then appoint others to do the rest of the work in the Church.

Here are some other Scriptures that point us to the **SET MAN** in the Old Testament.

Jeremiah 49:19 "Behold, he shall come up like a lion from the swelling of Jordan against the habitation of the strong: but I will suddenly make him run away from her: and who is a **CHOSEN M**an that I may **APPOINT** over her? …and who is that **SHEPHERD** that will stand before me?"

Isaiah 63:11 "Then he remembered the days of old, Moses, and his people, saying, Where is he that brought them up out of the sea with **SHEPHERD** of his flock?…"

Note that, in the Septuagint, the "chosen man", the "shepherd" is called **BISHOP** and it is used there to identify the Set Man.

CHAPTER TWO

MOSES AND JETHRO

When we look in the Old Testament and see Moses, we see the God's "Set Man". And, in this Scripture, Moses petitions The Lord concerning the Leader that is to be "appointed" over the Congregation… i.e. The Set Man.

Numbers 27:16-17 (ESV)

16 "Let the LORD, the God of the spirits of all flesh, **appoint a man over the congregation** who shall go out before them and come in before them, who shall lead them out and bring them in, that the congregation of the LORD may not be as sheep that have no shepherd."

Moses clearly mentions two things here and shows how important they are by making a "double annunciation" of them:

1. **GO OUT BEFORE THEM**
2. **GO IN BEFORE THEM**
3. **LEAD THEM OUT**
4. **BRING THEM IN**

The Set Man is the Leader who brings the people in and out just as a Shepherd leads his flock out to pasture and then leads them back to their corrals.

But, as we see very clearly, Moses was not perfect and made the same mistakes that the Leaders of Churches still make today. He tried to fill the role of the Set Man by being "Pastoral". Instead, he should have filled the role of the Set Man by being "Apostolic Role". He was trying to do everything himself! This is a very common problem in the Church today. Entire books and courses of study in seminaries have been written and taught which demonstrate the common belief that the "Pastor" is supposed to handle every aspect of Church life by himself. Moses was very blessed to have his father-in-law Jethro counsel him.

Exodus 18:19-27 (KJV)

Hearken now unto my voice, I will give thee counsel, and God shall be with thee: Be thou for the people to God-ward, that thou mayest bring the causes unto God: [20]And thou shalt teach them ordinances and laws, and shalt shew them the way wherein they must walk, and the work that they must do. [21]Moreover thou shalt provide out of all the people able men, such as fear God, men of truth, hating covetousness; and place *such* over them, *to be* rulers of thousands, *and* rulers of hundreds, rulers of fifties, and rulers of tens: [22]And let them judge the people at all seasons: and it shall be, *that* every great matter they shall bring unto thee, but every small matter they shall judge: so shall it be easier for thyself, and they shall bear *the burden* with thee. [23]If thou shalt do this thing, and God command thee *so*, then thou shalt be able to endure, and all this people shall also go to their place in peace. [24]So Moses hearkened to the voice of his father in law, and did all that he had said. [25]And Moses chose able men out

of all Israel, and made them heads over the people, rulers of thousands, rulers of hundreds, rulers of fifties, and rulers of tens.
26And they judged the people at all seasons: the hard causes they brought unto Moses, but every small matter they judged themselves.
27And Moses let his father in law depart; and he went his way into his own land.

The following things stand out in that passage:

1. He was God-ward and set his priorities in the Word of God and Prayer
2. He would Receive and Reveal God's Will
3. He would Demonstrate the power of God
4. He would be the one who would make decisions
5. He would Gather and Shepherd the people
6. He would Lead them out of bondage

M***oses tried to do all of this by himself which led to him becoming worn out and that had an effect on the people… They were getting worn out too! His solution was laid out by Jethro…***

THE JETHRO PRINCIPLE

Because Moses and the people were getting so weary the Lord sent his father-in-law Jethro to him to give him some sound leadership advice.

I've highlighted several things in this passage:

Exodus 18:19-21 "Hearken now unto my voice, I will give thee counsel..."

1. Be thou for the people to **GODWARD**
    a. that thou mayest bring the causes unto God
2. And thou shalt teach them ordinances and laws
    a. and shalt **SHOW THEM THE WAY** wherein they must walk
    b. **AND THE WORK** that they must do
3. Moreover thou shalt provide out of all the people able men
    a. such as **FEAR GOD**
    b. men of **TRUTH**
    c. hating **COVETOUSNESS**
4. **AND PLACE SUCH OVER THEM**
    a. to be rulers of thousands
    b. and rulers of hundreds
    c. rulers of fifties
    d. and rulers of tens
5. **AND LET THEM JUDGE THE PEOPLE AT ALL SEASONS**
    a. and it shall be, that **EVERY GREAT MATTER** they shall bring unto thee
    b. but every small matter they shall judge
    c. so shall it be easier for thyself
    d. and they shall **BEAR THE BURDEN** with thee.
6. If thou shalt do this thing, and God command thee so
    a. then thou shalt be able to endure
    b. and all this people shall also go to their place in peace

Because he himself was a wise man, Moses saw the wisdom in Jethro's words and put them into practice. Church Leaders today who want to have fruitful Churches would be wise to do so also.

THE SUCCESSOR

Another thing that the Set Man must need to do is to prepare for someone to take his place. The Set Man should train his Leaders and see who The Lord is putting His hand upon as a successor. There is a saying that the Lord spoke

to me years ago when I was learning and implementing these truths. I heard Him say to me:

"No man is a success unless he has a successor".

Moses saw that it was to be Joshua that would succeed him and the Lord confirmed it. So at the proper time Moses brought Joshua before all the people, laid hands on him and "**SET**" him into place as the new Leader of Israel. Joshua then became the next Set Man.

CHAPTER THREE

THE SET MAN IN THE CHURCH

In Crete Titus, one of Paul's Apostolic Team Members, was appointed as the Bishop of Crete; the Set Man. He was told by Paul to set everything in order and ordain elders who would follow in his footsteps as he had followed Paul's.

Titus 1:1-5 "…For this cause left I thee in Crete, that thou shouldest **SET IN ORDER** the things that are wanting, and **ORDAIN ELDERS** in every city, as I had appointed thee:

He first brought **GOVERNMENT** through the Jethro Principle: **TEACHING** and **TRAINING** then in order for the Church to avoid **LEGALISM,** relationships had to be built through **DISCIPLESHIP.**

JAMES, THE SET MAN AMONG THE APOSTLES

When the Apostles came to Jerusalem for the very first Apostolic Convocation it became very evident who they respected as their leader and under whose Authority they willingly submitted themselves. It was to James, the brother of the Lord, the Set Man of Jerusalem We can see this very clearly simply by the fact the it was the Apostle James who had the last word in the Apostolic Summit that was held and the where everyone agreed to it.

We can see this clearly in the **Book of Acts 15:13-19** "And after they had held their peace, James answered, saying, Men and brethren, hearken unto me… Wherefore **MY SENTENCE IS** that we trouble not them, which from among the Gentiles are turned to God:"

And one more point must be made for anyone who desires to be a leader. A person "in authority", must themselves be "under authority" as evidenced by the Apostles themselves.

THE CENTURION – A MAN UNDER AUTHORITY

Luke 7:8 (KJV)

"For I also am a man **SET UNDER AUTHORITY**, having under me soldiers, and I say unto one, Go, and he goes; and to another, Come, and he comes; and to my servant, Do this, and he does it."

Jesus marveled at the faith of the Centurion because that man understood **DELEGATED AUTHORITY**. He was an authority because he was "**SET UNDER AUTHORITY**".

Leaders in the Church have authority because they are under the Authority of the Set Man. When Leaders operate "under authority" it allows the anointing of the Holy Spirit to flow in the Church and it safeguards the flock from "wolves in sheep's clothing".

THE APOSTOLIC ROLE OF THE SET MAN

God is calling for a "**LEADER-SHIFT**" and he wants His **SET MEN** to take on more of an **APOSTOLIC ROLE** rather than to continue in the "**PASTORAL ROLE**" that they have been ministering in. This does not mean every Set Man will be an Apostle but rather that there will be a redefining of his function as the Leader of the Flock. The Set Man must develop a **PRESBYTERY OF ELDERS** over which he then functions as a **"BISHOP".**

Here are some of the main aspects for The Set Man to follow more of an "Apostolic Role":

- The Set Man must be "Godward" to carry the burden of the Lord
    - Too many are only concerned with the needs of the people
- The **SET MAN** must center on God's call and His purposes for the Church
    - This entails receiving Vision for his Church so he does not just "copy" what others are doing
- The **SET MAN** must raise up a **PRESBYTERY OF ELDERS**
    - This is the group that will minister to the people and their needs most of the time
- The Set Man must see that meeting the root needs of his Congregation is his primary concern
    - He must know the true needs of people and not just what

they think they need

- The **Set Man** must train his **Elders** and **Pastors**
    - These Leaders should focus on "feeding the sheep" Apostolic Doctrine
    - They must also "train" them in spiritual things so they will have their "spiritual muscles" built up

- The **Set Man** must look for and identify the potential that lies inherent within his flock
    - Then he must work with the Elders to create a means to develop those potentials

- We are living in a day when so many Leaders simply focus on a "bless me" type of service in which they try to meet their peoples' "felt needs"
    - In this "Leader-Shift" the **Set Man** must minister the Word of God and make a righteous demand of the people so they will become "doers of the Word and not hearers only"

- The **Set Man** must eliminate the "one man show" and instead build a **Ministry Team**
    - The members of the Ministry Team should each have some aspect of a 5 Fold Ministry gifting to help equip every believer so they may be led into their ministry

- The **SET MAN** must lead people into the fulfillment of God's will for them
  - Too many Pastors lead people to the same old place of trying to make them feel good and this does not lead to spiritual growth nor to an emotionally healthy life.

- The **SET MAN** must renew the minds of believers to see change in their lifestyles

- The **SET MAN** must move his **LEADERSHIP TEAM** out of a "maintenance" mentality
  - They must focus on the maturity of each individual

- The Set Man must also develop **THE CORPORATE IDENTITY** of the Church
  - This is so everyone can move forward in the same direction and advance the Kingdom of God

When the "Pastor" and the "Elders" have this vision the Church will move in the will of God and advance God's Kingdom on earth. Without this vision they just keep doing the same old thing..

Some good questions to ask yourself now are:

1. Is your Church moving in the Apostolic Vision of a Set Man?

2. Do you see yourself functioning "under authority" by being accountable to another Man of God?
3. Are you being helped to come into your ministry gifting?
4. Would you say that the Pastor in your Church functions more as a "Pastor" or as an "Apostolic Leader"?
5. Is there a Ministry Team in place in your Church?
6. Are you a part of that Team?
7. Can you say that your Church is an "Apostolic Church" functioning under the Leadership of an Apostolic Set Man?

CHAPTER FOUR

WHAT IS A LEADER?

I am going to put forth a simple explanation of what a Leader is. To some this might be oversimplified but after you read this I think you will agree that a simple explanation is fitting.

A Leader is a person who has two things in particular…

1. They have Influence
2. They have the Ability to get Followers

Not every Leader is a great Charismatic person. Many times a Leader does not stand out in a crowd. They may not be good looking. They might not have the greatest command of language. They may be a plain as any plain Jane or Joe could be.

True Leaders have knowledge and experience in the area they are leading in. And, it is that knowledge and experience that creates Influence. When a person is marked as an influential person other people are attracted to them. And, among those who are attracted will be those who become their followers.

True Leaders are never great because of externals… They are great because they have the heart and the calling to Lead and that passion flows somehow through them. That is another thing that gives them the ability to get Followers.

It is simply these specific things that give someone the ability to become a great Leader. Whether they become a great Leader in the Church will depend on one more thing; their relationship with God. Without that they can never be “great”. Even if they have large followings they will not be great in God’s eyes and it is His opinion that counts for eternity!

What else is a Leader? Here are two practical things that a Leader may be. A Leader may be a person who acts as a Guide or a Conductor. Let’s define these words for our use:

A Guide is a person who may do any of these things:

1. They direct another person’s conduct
2. They direct another person’s course of life
3. They are a person who exhibits and/or explains points of interest
4. They are a member of a unit on whom the movements or alignments of a military command are regulated

***A Conductor** may be or do any of these things*

1. Be the leader of a musical ensemble
2. Be the first or principal performer of a group
3. A horse placed in advance of the other horses of a team
4. A material or object that permits an electric current to flow thru it easily
5. A material that is capable of transmitting another form of energy such as heat or sound

Here are a couple of salient thoughts:
If you aspire to be a leader then you would be responsible for directing another's life (or at least a part of it). And the greatest place to direct people to is a relationship with Jesus. You would have to get to know a lot about The Bible so you could point out things of interest in it. Looking at the aspect of a Conductor you should strive to be a person through whom the Anointing of The Holy Spirit can flow through so that the power of The Holy Spirit may touch and bless others.

And so looking at these possibilities we can then apply them to our lives and become a Leader!

Chapter Five

The 5 levels of Leadership

Adapted from John Maxwell's book: Developing the Leader Within You

John Maxwell discovered that there are five distinct levels of Leadership. As a Leader you need to understand these 5 levels of Leadership and then make them a reality in your life.

1. **Position**: This is based on rights and although this is the lowest level of Leadership it is still very valid. Children and young people need these Leaders in their lives simply because they provide a constant that brings security and purpose. Others need this type of Leadership in their lives because it can give them a form of discipline necessary for creating a successful mind set towards tasks. In this level people follow you
   a. Because of your title or position
   b. "Because you said so or simply because you're the boss

The problem here is that your influence will not extend beyond your job description. And, consequently, the longer you stay here the higher the turnover and the lower the morale of those you lead will become.

2. **Permission**: This secondary level of Leadership is based upon relationships. This is a higher level than Position because people give you "Permission" to lead them. This creates an

additional responsibility upon the Leader and should help them grow into the next level. In this level people follow you because they want to.
The problem with staying at this level too long is that it causes highly motivated people to leave and go elsewhere. That can create lack in the Church because the ones that should be fulfilling a part of the Church Vision have now left.

3. **Production**: This next level is based on results and is the first level that does not really have a downside. When you function at this level people see what you have done for the Church and are impressed to stay and become fruitful followers.
A big plus on this level is that it helps to build momentum in the Church in both the individual spiritual growth of the members and in the programs and outreach of the Church.

4. **People Development**: When you reach this level you will see yourself reproduced in the lives of those who are actively following you. This is a very rewarding level and again, this level has no real downside.
a. As you attain this level of Leadership you will find that Church Members follow you because of what you have done for them. They become very faithful to you and to the Church.
b. On this level long-range growth occurs and a legacy is formed
The major benefit this level has is that the Church Members become

extremely loyal to you and the Church. This creates a great sense of community and even family among the Members.

5. **<u>Personhood</u>**: This final level is based upon the respect that you have earned among those who follow you. This is the ultimate goal of a great Leader. This level of Leadership brings the greatest amount of satisfaction to the Leader and it brings tremendous value to those who follow. They are empowered simply because you are their Leader and they love you. This level is attained because you have created and maintained a proven track record. Now your Church Members follow you because of who and what you represent; Jesus Christ and The Kingdom of God.

There are several important things to remember here:

1. You are really never on the same level with everyone in a group
2. You never really leave the base level; instead you build upon it
3. You should never try to skip a level. That would affect your long-range goals
4. You need to know what level you are on with the people you influence in order to be most effective.

Chapter Six

Five Leadership Skills

Now that you have a good working definition of what a Leader is and you've seen the 5 levels of Leadership you are ready to look at 5 Leadership Skills. Remember, you're not just reading this for knowledge; you want to understand these so you can apply them to your own life and role as a Leader.

The first level is that of a ***Facilitator***. A Facilitator is a person who skillfully creates an atmosphere that is conducive to building relationships. They will use ideas, images and words that cast a vision or paint a picture of where they want to go. A Facilitator may also be someone who assists or guides people through a process making it flow easily and smoothly. Remember this; a Facilitator is not necessarily called to "teach" people but is called to assist people in the process of "self-realization" making them productive, fruitful people in the Kingdom of God.

Re-read the Gospels and look at the life of Jesus trying to see how he filled the role of a Facilitator in his relationship building with his Disciples.

The second level is that of the ***Shepherd***. Here are two Scriptures that show us that role:

1 Peter 5:2 (NLT)

"Care for the flock that God has entrusted to you. Watch over it willingly, not grudgingly—not for what you will get out of it, but because you are eager to serve God."

1 Thessalonians 5:14 (NLT)
"Brothers and sisters, we urge you to warn those who are lazy. Encourage those who are timid. Take tender care of those who are weak. Be patient with everyone."

The things that stand out in these two exhortative Scriptures are that a Shepherd must be willing and also be available to spend some time with his people. This demonstrates the heart of a Shepherd. They believe that they are serving The Lord by serving His people.

Shepherds are also sensitive to the physical, emotional and spiritual needs of people. They are able to warn people without scaring them. They are tender towards the weak and are patient with others because they have allowed the nature of Christ to be worked into their own lives. These qualities will continually grow within you as you continual to place those under you first.

The third level is that of a ***Mentor***. This type of Leader is a counselor and a guide and may function as a tutor.

A Mentor stays close enough to those under their tutelage to keep track of their spiritual growth. Because a Mentor is usually older they are able to draw upon their experiences and help their mentee(s) avoid situations that would hinder their spiritual growth. They are close enough to continually encourage them to follow the path The Lord is presenting to them.

Fourth is the ***Planner***. This is the type of Leader sees the future and plans, prays and perseveres.

This is a person who says things like: "If you fail to plan you plan to fail." Because they have "Studied to show themselves approved" they are "workmen that need not be ashamed rightly dividing the Word of Truth".

Another thing, which is a great safeguard to those they lead is that they are able to teach them not to plan things to death.

The Planner is able to impart this important truth as they create plans; People want to follow a person who knows where they are going.

Last, there is the ***Mobilizer***. The Mobilizer is a Leader who is secure in their own role and is able to bring people to the point where they are "released" into their own servant roles.

The Mobilizer demonstrates this thru Delegation. They don't release people into their own too soon because they are able to evaluate properly and release people properly. By doing this they affirm their followers This is the person who is able to bring correction for growth and reaffirm them too as time goes by.

To help you develop your skills ask yourself and ask others who know you well the following question…

"Which one of these in the skillset I normally operate in?"

Chapter Seven

Three Leadership Styles

Although we can find many variations of Leadership styles I feel that these three stand out among all others. For each of these three let's look at the following:

The Type An Example The Earmarks

Type: **CONTROL/COMMAND**
Example: This is the WWII Military Style
Earmarks: Loyalty

Type: **CEO**
Example: These people Communicate Vision
Earmarks: Partners
Church Growth
People buy into the vision
Mega Church Movement

Type: **COACH**
Example: Resonance– Listening, Responding and Reinforcing
Earmarks: Commitment
Emotionally Healthy Leadership
Personal Growth of Individuals
Team Growth and a Corporate Culture
One size does not fit all

Uniqueness of the individual valued

Moral Motivation

Iron Sharpening Iron

Which is the Style that you see Jesus using?

In my mind there is one particular Scripture that points us to Jesus' methodology…

Mark 3:14 Then He appointed twelve, that they might be with Him and that He might send them out to preach,

Jesus' first goal as a Leader was to have those that followed Him "be with Him"

There is simply no better way for someone to learn and to grow spiritually then to be able to spend precious time with their Leaders. By spending time with him his Disciples were able to see how he did things. Many times his Disciples did not understand him and later on they would ask him why he did what he did. Sending them out to preach was not his number one priority… that they would "be with him" was.

This is one of the reasons why I believe that Jesus acted mostly as a Coach using Resonance. Let's look at Resonance and then we'll look at one of the most powerful examples of it in the Bible.

Resonance: Although we find him using the other two at times, this was the way He created Disciples and molded Leaders. Rather than sounding a note (casting vision or commanding) you listen for the note in the individual and then respond to that note: reinforcing it, strengthening it, confirming it and empowering it!

A definition of Resonance:

An amplification of a sound, e.g. that of an instrument or the human voice, caused by sympathetic vibration in a chamber such as an auditorium or a singer's chest

An increased amplitude of oscillation of a mechanical system when it is subjected to vibration from another source at or near its own natural frequency

Application of Resonance:

Jesus would discover the underlying sound that The Lord God placed in the heart of each individual and then He would produce that sound within Himself amplifying it within the person. This resulted in the sound within the person becoming strong and true.

To a Coach, life is a classroom. Coaches are able to recognize and take advantage of "***Teachable Moments***". So, let's see Jesus, the Coach, creating a "teachable moment" that demonstrates this truth with His declaration that He is The Messiah.

Matthew 16:13-18 (ESV) "Now when Jesus came into the district of Caesarea Philippi, he asked his disciples, "Who do people say that the Son of Man is?" And they said, "Some say John the Baptist, others say Elijah, and others Jeremiah or one of the prophets." He said to them, "But who do you say that I am?" Simon Peter replied, "You are the Christ, the Son of the living God." And Jesus answered him, "Blessed are you, Simon Bar-Jonah! For flesh and blood has not revealed this to you, but my Father who is in heaven. And I tell you, you are Peter, and on this rock I will build my church, and the gates of hell shall not prevail against it."

This is the first time Jesus reveals that He is The Christ (Messiah). He also talks about the Church's foundation and the fact that the "gates of hell" cannot prevail against the Church. These are, without a doubt, three of the most important revelations Jesus ever gave to his disciples.

What we don't see is the "Coach" at work here creating a "teachable moment" and using Resonance to drive his message home! Why? Because we don't know the "context" within which He made these revelations. So, let's look at this together…

In order to get to Caesarea Philippi, which lay at the foot of Mt. Hermon, Jesus took his disciples on a 30 mile plus hike into a place that the Rabbis of his day considered one of the most sinful places in the land! This city was the "Sodom and Gomorrah" of Jesus' day!

Here sat the Temple of Pan. You should recognize Pan. He was the god who was half man and half goat. He was the god of shepherds and fertility. But here is something you may not have known. His name, Pan, is the root of the word "panic" because he was also the god who instilled fear into people!

At this temple site the followers of Pan would hold drunken orgies as they worshipped him. There was a huge niche in the rock wall there where there stood a huge erotic statue of Pan playing his flute. There, along the roadside, were several other smaller niches with statues of Pan's nymphs… his sex partners.

In order to make the declaration of his Messiahship as bold and as clear as possible Jesus creates the sharpest contrast possible for His disciples. He is "The Good Shepherd", the "Prince of Peace". Pan is the god of shepherds who struck fear in the hearts of men and who encouraged licentiousness and outright sexual deviation and orgies as the god of fertility. Jesus, on the other hand promoted holiness as the seed of His Kingdom's fertile growth!

Pan's temple was built at the foot of Mt. Hermon one of the most important mountains in all of the Promised Land. It was here that modern scholars believe that Jesus was transfigured and spoke with Moses and Elijah. The solid rock of the temple's foundation stood there in contrast to Jesus's statement about Peter's confession of faith in Jesus as "The Christ; the Son of the Living God" and His saying that "on this Rock I will build my Church"!

This brings us to the next part of Jesus' statement… "And the gates of hell shall not prevail against it"!

Jesus wraps up this powerful teachable moment as he stands with His disciples in front of a cave that was known as "the gates of hell"!

Here, in the face of Pan, Jesus is revealed as "The Christ". It is here that He says He will build His Church on this confession of Faith and it is here, in front of the gates of hell that He declares that they shall not be able to stand against His Church!

It was by bringing His disciples here that He was able to speak words that would vibrate inside of them and "resonate"! They resonated so much within Peter that he boldly declared: "You are The Christ, the Son of The Living God!"

When Jesus spoke to His disciples that day His words "resonated" or "vibrated" within them. His words touched them deep inside and released the sound of true in their souls.

A Coach looks for "teachable moments" because "actions speak louder than words". Can you see Jesus standing in from of the statue of the god Pan and asking: "Whom do men say I am?"

Can you see Jesus turning to the crowds of Pans orgiastic followers and worshippers and declaring that His Church would be filled with His holy followers and then, pointing to the cave where those ungodly people worshipped their "false" shepherd sex god and declaring that the very gates of hell would never prevail against His Church!

What a day! What do you think the discussions were around the campfires that evening???

While it is true that Leaders today must learn to use the Command/Control and CEO style of Leadership when needed they MUST DEVELOP a "listening ear" to hear what is within those they serve and then speak things that will resonate within them. This will bring those people to a place of security and then to the place of deep personal commitment to their Leader. This is the highest form of Leadership.

This is Servant Leadership...

For us to implement this type of Servant Leadership our methodology has to be wo pronged:

1. We **must listen** to the heart of another
2. We **must ask**: "How can I serve you?"

When we share the deep truths that our followers need to hear in this manner they will never forget them. And, they will never forget the Leader who shared them… you!

Chapter Eight

Leadership and Management

(In the Church setting)

The story has been told about a group of tourists who were visiting a picturesque village. As they walked by an old man sitting beside a fence one tourist asked in a patronizing way, "Were any great men born in this village?" The old man replied, "No, only babies."

There are very few leadership books. Even if they have "leadership" in the title most of them deal with management. There seems to be a great deal of confusion over the difference between leadership and management.

Management is the process of assuring that the program and objectives of the organization are implemented. Leadership, on the other hand, has to do with casting vision and motivating people.

Someone has said: "People don't want to be managed. They want to be led. Whoever heard of a world manager? World leader, yes; Education leader, yes; Political leader; Religious leader; Scout leader; Community leader; Labor leader; Business leader; Yes. They lead. They don't manage. The carrot always wins over the stick. Ask your horse. You can lead your horse to water, but you can't *manage* him to drink."

If you want to manage somebody, manage yourself!

***Leadership* is influence and the ability to get followers**

***Management* is the planning, implementation and ongoing support of the vision of the Leader**

Let's look at these in The Church understanding something very important; You need BOTH Leaders and Managers in the Church!

I. **A Leader in Church - The Apostolic Set Man**

a. The Leader is the Visionary
b. The Leader Inspires and Sets Direction
c. The Leader Communicates the Vision
d. The Leader Creates a Picture of the future
e. Leaders Motivate people through Giftings and Charisma
f. A Leader Builds Understanding
g. The Leaders Energizes others through their Personality
h. Leaders Enable others through Listening

II. **A Manager is Church terms: The Pastor or an Elder**

a. A Manager Implements The Set Man's Vision
b. A Manager Builds Staff
c. Managers Create plans and systems
d. A Manager Organizes
e. A Manager Budgets expenses
f. Managers Report back to Leaders
g. A Manager solves problems
h. A Manager creates continuity and flow in the Church

Chapter Nine

PREPARING LEADERS

In raising up His leaders Jesus was very focused…
His ministry to multitudes in preaching, healing, etc. was not his main emphasis; they were like rest stops on the journey to raising up leaders. We see this in what is called The Pareto Principle.

Spend 80% of your time with 20% of your people

A Leader must determine who it is that God has given you to work with and then spend the majority of you time working with them. Don't let the "***squeaky wheel***" get your oil!

Another thing is that you must recognize that you can really only effectively train about 12 people. That's why the Apostle Paul told Timothy two things in ***2 Timothy 2:2*** "And the things that thou hast heard of me among many witnesses, the same

(1) **commit thou to faithful men**,

(2) **who shall be able to teach others also**."

Don't let you goal to be "collect people" but rather to "select people" and give everything to them!

John 2:23-24 says: [23]Now when he was in Jerusalem at the Passover, in the feast day, many believed in his name, when they

saw the miracles which he did. ***But Jesus did not commit himself unto them***, because he knew all men…"
So, Jesus did not "commit" himself to everyone He ministered to even it they believed in Him.

Jo***hn 17:6*** says: "I have manifested thy name ***unto the men which thou gave me*** out of the world: thine they were, and thou gave them me; and they have kept thy word.
Here, once again, we can see that Jesus worked with the 12 whom God had given to Him to work with.

Here is another part of choosing who to work with. ***Luke 10:2*** says: "Therefore said he unto them, The harvest truly is great, but the laborers few: pray ye therefore the Lord of the harvest, that he would send forth laborers into his harvest."
You need to make sure that you find "Laborers" too. If you get them and you'll get revival in your Church.

Challenge those whom God has given to you to follow you and as they follow you mentor and train them. Your Key Followers, those who are the Next Generation's Leaders must fit the advice of Paul to Timothy… They must be faithful men who are committed to you just as much as you are committed to them.

In ***Mark 1:17*** Jesus said to the disciples: "**Come after me**, and **I will make you become** fishers of men."

The Five Steps of Preparing Leaders

1) ***Identify:*** What Fivefold Gifting do they possess?

Ephesians 4:7 says: "But unto every one of us is given grace according to the measure of ***the gift of Christ***."

You need The Holy Spirit to reveal their gift and calling to you and then you need to spend time with them to confirm what you "heard" from God.

2) ***Affirm***: Speak positively into their life

In **John 1:22** Jesus changed Peter's name to fit his identity and calling. In the same manner you need to speak to them about who and what they are becoming.

3) ***Impart***: Pour your gifts into them

Romans 1:11 says: "For I long to see you, that I may impart unto you some spiritual gift, to the end ye may be established." Lay hands on them, teaching, counseling, fellowshipping and caring for them will not only impart what you have into them but it will seal it inside of them and place in them the understanding of "passing the baton" to the next generation when it is their turn to Lead.

4) ***Activate***: Let them get their feet wet

Matthew 14:28-31 says: "And Peter answered him and said, Lord, if it be thou, bid me come unto thee on the water. And he said, Come. And when Peter was come down out of the ship, he walked on the water, to go to Jesus. But when he saw the wind boisterous, he was afraid; and beginning to sink, he cried, saying, Lord, save me." Even if Jesus had known that Peter was going to sink I believe He still would have called him out to walk on the water and get his feet wet! You do this when you delegate some responsibilities to them; even if they are bigger than they can handle. Then, after they have gotten their feet wet sit with them and do some critical analysis of their results. Look at what Jesus did in ***Matthew 14:-31*** **"**And immediately Jesus stretched forth *his* hand, and caught him, and said unto him, O thou of little faith, ***wherefore didst thou doubt***?" Contrary to what most people think, Jesus did not cut Peter down with that question. The Greek shows us that He probably said that with a smile calling him a "little-faith". In other words, He was bringing Peter's attention more to the walking on water rather than the sinking!

5) ***Release***: Consecrate them through a "Sending" Ceremony

Luke 10:1 says: After these things the Lord appointed other seventy also***, and sent them*** two and two before his face into every city and place, whither he himself would come. He made a point to "commission them" for their mission. After you send them out you have to continue their on-going training too. Look at what Jesus did in ***Luke 10:17-20***: "***And the seventy returned*** again with joy, saying, Lord, even the devils are subject unto us through thy name. [18]***And he said unto them***, I beheld Satan as lightning fall from heaven. [19]Behold, I give unto you power to tread on serpents and scorpions, and over all the power of the enemy: and nothing shall by any means hurt you. [20]Notwithstanding in this rejoice not, that the spirits are subject unto you; but rather rejoice, because your names are written in heaven.".

Chapter Ten

Successful Leadership

If you do a little critical analysis of the Great Commission you would be able to hear Jesus say it this way:

"I will build my church - you go and make disciples..."

We become Successful Leaders by discipling others. This is what is known as Apprenticeship. Here are three key Scriptures…

Mark 3:13-14 "And he went up to a mountaintop, and he called those whom he had chosen and they came unto him. And he ordained twelve, **that they should be with him**, and that he might send them forth to preach."

Psalm 103:7 "He made known **his ways** unto Moses, **his acts** unto the children of Israel."

Ezekiel 34:1-4 "And the word of the LORD came unto me, saying, Son of man, prophesy against the shepherds of Israel, and say unto them; 'Thus saith the Lord GOD unto the shepherds; Woe to the shepherds of Israel… You have not strengthened the diseased, neither have you healed the sick. You have not bound up the broken or brought back those that driven away and you have not gone looking for those which were lost'."

Here are the key points in these three Scriptures

1. Learn God's ways and then lead His sheep in His ways; become an Apprentice
2. Ask The Lord for compassion, understanding and the ability to reach out to backslidden and lost sheep
3. Leaders need to receive inner healing; wounded leaders wound others
4. Learn how to minister forgiveness and hope
5. Leaders have to know how to illuminate the process of "death to self"; the process where the Lord refines us like silver

When you have grown through the process of Apprenticeship/Discipleship God's sheep will be able to trust you to bring them into the process of Apprenticeship/Discipleship.

Here is a key truth to being a successful leader…

To be a Successful Leader you must Know Your People

John 17:4 & 12 "I have finished the work you gave me to do… I have not lost anyone that you have given me"

The first question therefore to start to fulfill the first rule of true leadership is; "Who has God given me to lead /shepherd?"

Even if you lead a large group you will still have a small core of people that God has given to you. Therefore, rethink your group to get to the smallest size… 3 or 4 and consider them as the ones that God has given you. To work with a small group and to Lead/Shepherd them there are just a few dynamics that come into play as you are building your relationships with your key followers.

1. What is the condition of your people?
    a. What work are they doing in the Church?
    b. How are they handling it?
2. Take a personal interest in your people…
    a. How is their home life?
    b. How is their work life?
    c. Are there areas of special concern that they have?
3. What skills do they possess?
    a. How can they use them for the Lord's work?
4. What are their interests?
5. What are their career goals?
6. What are their personal dreams?

Leading people is a simple and yet profound thing to accomplish. You build real, lasting relationships with your people when you:

1. Engage them on a regular basis
2. Spend time together with them
3. Talk to them on the phone
4. Write to them

5. Always ask a lot of personal questions and always listen.

Remember, your assignment is to ask the Lord to show you whom He has given to you in our Church or circle of influence.

So, who has He given you?

If you draw a blank it may be because the Lord has not given anyone to you and that's OK right now. You're still learning!

Now, whether you hear from God and know who He has given you or if you have not been given anyone yet, you must ask The Lord what essentially is the most important question you can ask Him concerning Leadership/Shepherding…

"Who have you given me to?"

Remember, you have to be "A man under authority" to have authority!

After you complete this exercise you need to see the Set Man God has given you to and discuss what you have discovered with them.

Chapter Eleven

Why Concentrate on Relationships?

Jesus ministered to large crowds and had a tremendous healing ministry BUT he never discipled the crowds. What we can see in the Gospel stories is that Jesus did his most important work with people "***one on one***" and in "***small groups***". This is where he reproduced himself.

While he was working in the healing ministry he cleansed 10 lepers but only one came back to thank him.

While he was discipling his primary small group he worked with 12 people. 11 became great leaders and only 1 fell away…

What do you think had the better results between the two? Healing ministry or Discipling ministry? With this truth exemplified in Jesus' own ministry we still find that a "Healing Ministry" still captures the imagination of many and it is seen by them as the way to build the Church. Let's look at the motivation behind this pattern of thinking.

What motivates people to seek a healing ministry?

If it is not the fulfillment of The Great Commission; "Go and make Disciples out of all Nations" then there must be an honest examination of our motives. I have found from experience (my own included) that there five major reasons why Men and Women of God desire to have a strong Healing Ministry.

The first one is COMPASSION. This is in most cases the primary motive to seek a Healing Ministry. The problem is that is it usually not the reason why, once in it, Ministers continue to build a bigger and bigger healing ministry.

After compassion has run its course and ceased to be the primary purpose PRIDE steps up and begins to lead the way to a bigger ministry. Let's be real. Success feels good and that's the breeding ground for Pride to grow stronger and stronger.

The third motivator is POWER. Again, being real… Power feels good too. But I'm sure you've heard the old adage: "Power tends to corrupt and absolute power corrupts absolutely." Once a man gets used to the taste of power they usually become addicted to it. That's why "Power tends to corrupt".

The fourth motivator that slips into the forefront is FAME. Want to keep it real? Fame feels good! Once a person get recognition everywhere they go and are placed in prominent positions over and over again Fame feeds the flame of their desire and now takes the lead position. It's not that the other motivators go away… they just fall in line and add to the strength of what has now become, for the most part, a carnal desire to see their Healing Ministry grow more and more. What was born out of compassion is now a mixture of godly and selfish motives.

Lastly, the fifth motivator is unleashed… MONEY! King Solomon said it so well in Ecclesiastes 10:19 "A feast is made for laughter, And wine makes merry; But money answers everything."

Here's a more literal way of saying that: "A party will make you laugh and wine will get you giddy but money talks and is the answer to everything".

Money feeds carnality like nothing else! Pride, Power and Fame create an atmosphere that simply cannot resist the flow of Money that comes into the Healing Ministry.

A careful study of the most famous healing ministries of the 19th and 20th centuries you will find that there are very few that were able to resist the power of these four corruptors. And Money seems to be the one that empowers a person more than any of the other three because it is used as a "proof" that God is behind the ministry.

I realize that this chapter has been dark but I believe this is a topic that must be talked about so we can put the enemy under our feet never giving in to the lure of these snares. This is a necessary conversation because too many Ministers begin their ministry out of Compassion but that is often sidetracked as the other four take over.

What motivates someone to build their ministry relationally placing the making of disciples paramount?

As I said at the beginning of this chapter, it is Compassion. The overwhelming feeling that makes us want to take care of people and do what is best for them. This can only continue to remain the top motivator if these next three motivators are added to it.

The first is SERVANTHOOD. When the desire for position reared its head among His disciples Jesus answered it. Read **Mark 10:35-45** for the full context but let's look at **Mark 10:43 (NKJV)** "But so shall it not be among you: but whosoever will be great among you, shall be your servant:". Placing others in Ministry above yourself and serving them will help you keep Compassion as your chief motivator.

The next motivator that will keep your ministry on the right track is simply known as "DYING TO SELF". Here we need to take a look at Jesus' way of thinking and the Apostle Paul most clearly tells us that is in Philippians 2:3-5 (NKJV) "Let nothing be done through selfish ambition or conceit, but in lowliness of mind let each esteem others better than himself. Let each of you look out not only for his own interests, but also for the interests of others. Let this mind be in you which was also in Christ Jesus..."

Paul brings several things to bear here as he aptly describes the "Mind of Christ"…

1. Selfish ambition crucified
2. Conceit crucified
3. Lowliness of Mind / Humility exalted
4. The interests of others placed ahead of your own
5. Esteem others as better than oneself

These are the earmarks of a Servant. And, as much as Paul tells us what it is Jesus himself SHOWS us through a "Teachable Moment". Look at the Gospel of John chapter 13:1-17 This is where Jesus takes a towel and wraps it around his waist and proceeds to wash his disciples feet. He then says to them in **John 13:13-15 (KJV)** "Ye call me Master and Lord: and ye say well; for *so* I am. If I then, *your* Lord and Master, have washed your feet; ye also ought to wash one another's feet. For I have given you an example, that ye should do as I have done to you."

Servanthood is real only when it washes the feet of others.

The third motivator is the DESIRE TO SEE THE KINGDOM OF GOD ESTABLISHED rather than your own. The good of the Church most always precede success for our ministry. If we don't keep the Kingdom first we will end up having built our own.

In my early years of ministry I wanted to see people's lives changed and I longed to see people healed of sicknesses and disease but as "my ministry" grew I had to face the four false motivators… Pride, Power, Fame and Money. I tried to preach "the Full Gospel" and so I preached about healings and miracles and I also spoke about dying to self. As I preached on healings and miracles I saw the Hand of God move and there were many testimonies… Cancer was removed by prayer, deafness was cured, crippling arthritis left at the command of faith. These were just a few of the signs and wonders that took place.

I've actually still got a scrap book of newspaper clippings and pictures along with personal testimonies. And, the more we saw God's Hand move the more people came to the Church. We were packed week after week. Prophecies were given that "This place is not big enough for what God wants to do." I saw a bigger building, a more prominent ministry through radio and TV and more money in the offerings every week!

Then, one day, The Lord spoke to me about preaching on "Dying to Self". So, I began to "Preach the Cross"! I blasted self and all that goes along with it and less and less people came to Church. Wait a minute, I thought. If I keep preaching "Dying to Self" and "The Cross" my Church is going to get smaller rather than bigger. I made up my mind that I wasn't going to preach it any more…

So, I prayed for healings and miracles; signs and wonders. I read everything I could on the subject to build my faith and still God spoke to me that I needed to preach the Cross. I told him I wouldn't do it. The people needed to be healed. The Church had to grow. We needed more money in the offerings to start to save to buy a bigger building.

But... The Holy Spirit was relentless! He took me to **Jeremiah 20:9 (KJV)** "Then I said, I will not make mention of him, nor speak any more in his name. But his word was in mine heart as a burning fire shut up in my bones, and I was weary with forbearing, and I could not stay."

He won! I had that "fire shut up in my bones" and I could not help but preach it!

Well, it had the effect that I knew would happen. Less and less new people came out. We stopped growing and shrunk instead. But, even though I knew I was not pleasing the people, I was pleasing God and that made all the difference!

Instead of "the fastest growing Church" around we became a place where Disciples are formed and Jesus Christ is Lord. I was determined that I would never hear these words from Jesus' mouth: **Matthew 7:22-23 (KJV)** "Many will say to me in that day, Lord, Lord, have we not prophesied in thy name? and in thy name have cast out devils? and in thy name done many wonderful works? And then will I profess unto them, I never knew you: depart from me, ye that work iniquity."

No, I was determined to build my house on the Rock and not sand.

How about you?

Chapter Twelve

TEAMWORK & DISCIPLESHIP

There are no Lone Rangers… even he had Tonto as his companion.

We all admire achievers:

Business Leaders:	Sam Walton, Bill Gates
Athletes:	Mickey Mantle, Michael Jordan
Artists:	Picasso, Michelangelo, Mozart
Spiritual Leaders:	John Wesley, Billy Graham
Political Leaders:	Alexander the Great, Ronald Reagan
Great Thinkers:	Thomas Edison, Albert Einstein

We Americans love pioneers and bold individualism BUT the truth is that no one person ever achieves anything great alone… there are always others involved in the background somewhere.

Einstein was heard to say: "Many times a day I realize how much my own outer and inner life is built upon the labors of my fellow men, both living and dead, and how earnestly I must exert myself in order to give in return as much as I have received."

Wagons trains conquered the west… men working in assembly lines changed the worlds industry… a team of men and women put a man on the moon but American mythology still extols the individual. In

America we have Halls of Fame for so many activities but nowhere do we have a Hall of Fame for Teamwork.

President Lyndon Johnson said: "There are no problems that we cannot solve together, and very few that we can solve by ourselves."

Teams afford more resources, ideas and energy than one individual.
Teams maximize a leader's potential and minimize their weaknesses.
Teams are able to devise multiple perspectives for setting and meeting goals.
Teams share credit and blame thus creating true humility and community.
Teams keep leaders accountable.
Teams can just do more than an individual!

Why do we still want to idolize individuals who stand alone since teams can do so much? Here are some of the reasons why…

1. **EGO**: Steel magnate and Philanthropist Andrew Carnegie (Founder of US Steel) said: "It marks a big step in your development when you come to realize that other people can help you do a better job than you could do alone."

2. **INSECURITY**: Insecure leaders either want to control

everything around them or they fear being replaced by someone who does things better than they do.

3. **NAIVETÉ**: Some leaders fail to understand the difficulty of achieving great things and fail to ask for help.

4. **TEMPERAMENT**: Some people simply aren't outgoing and just don't think in terms of teams.

President Woodrow Wilson said: "We should not only use all the brains we have, but all that we can borrow."

One is too small a number to achieve greatness.

Discipleship And Apprenticeship

If Church were a sport what would you consider to be "winning"?

a. Saving souls
b. Making disciples
c. Both

The answer, of course, is both. You can't make disciples if you don't save souls! But, what then is a disciple? It's our understanding of discipleship that will give us the desire we need to do whatever we have to do against any and all odds.

Discipleship has different levels… It's like apprenticeship in a craft or art.

A Master Craftsman would take on an apprentice who would study under the Master Craftsman. The Apprentice or his parents would pay the Master to learn a trade. Meanwhile the Master would provide food and shelter for the Apprentice. After a while, if the Apprentice had the necessary skill he would become a Journeyman… a skilled worker who could be employed. A Journeyman might continue to work for his Master or he could look to work for any Master who wanted to hire him.

In Medieval times each Craft was overseen by a Guild. In order for a Journeyman to become a Master he would have to submit a sample of his work to the Guild for approval. If they approved he would be admitted into the Guild and be recognized as a Master Craftsman and be able to take on Apprentices of his own. He could open a shop and have his own business.

Doesn't this sound like the type of person Paul was? Remember when he referred to himself as a "Master Architect"? He was someone who had achieved a certain level of excellence and was in the process of training others like Timothy and Titus to one day take his role! Apprenticeship demonstrates Discipleship in action!

Chapter Thirteen

The Church as a "Craft"

Making disciples is a lot like the Guild System of Medieval times. Jesus uses two metaphors to describe "Church"…

1. We are supposed to be "fishers of men" and after catching them we must clean them up which is the process of bringing wholeness to their souls.
2. We are supposed to be shepherds taking care of sheep which implies nurturing them and keeping them free from disease so they can reproduce healthy sheep.

And, it takes a "team" to do either one of these things.

The question then is this: Do you want to be on this team?

If our answer is yes then we must start off as apprentices learning our trade:

1. Catching and cleaning fish
2. Shepherding and nurturing sheep

However you look at it we've got some learning to do. Let's apply the Guild metaphor to this process. Making disciples is a lot like the Guild System of Medieval times. The Set Man is like the Master Craftsman. His apprentices are believers whom he trains in the ways of the Lord. As they progress from being hearers of the word and become doers of the word they become Disciples; the equivalent of a Journeyman.

As I mentioned previously, each Craft was overseen by a Guild and in order for a Journeyman to become a Master Craftsman he would have to submit a sample of his work to the Guild for approval. If they approved he would be admitted into the Guild and be recognized as a Master Craftsman and he could open a shop of his own and take on apprentices of his own..

The true purpose of the Guild was to keep the quality of a craft or trade at the highest level possible. All the Master Craftsmen (Set Men) knew each other and held each other accountable to the proper standards. As they did this each Master was able to have a profitable business.

If we did the same thing in the Church world we would have quality Churches filled with people who want the best for the Church rather than for themselves and everyone would benefit.

Think of the Master (the Set Man) as part of a Guild (a Church Network). He takes on Apprentices (believers both old and new) and he trains them in his craft (in the ways of the Lord). They progress from learners to doers and become Journeyman (Deacons and Ministers). Once they have achieved that level they may, should they feel so inclined after approval by the Guild (Ordination), set up a shop (plant a Church) of their own.

The Guild was a Team… do you want to be a player on our Church Team or do you want to strike out on your own… be a Lone Ranger. If you want to be on the Team then you have to become an Apprentice.

Looking at The Church as a Guild

If we look at the Church as a Guild we would see the following…

The Apprentice	=	***An Emerging Leader***
The Journeyman	=	***A Deacon or Elder***
The Master Craftsman	=	***The Set Man***

I think we need to start over and ask the Lord to take us to new levels of understanding so that He, as the Master of all Craftsmen, can boast about us and the work we do for His Kingdom.

Chapter Fourteen

The Listening Leader

One of the basics that Leaders must have is the ability to listen…

There are Three Basic Listening Modes

1. **Competitive** or **Combative Listening** This is what happens when we are more interested in promoting our own point of view than in understanding or exploring someone else's. We either listen for openings to take the floor, or for flaws or weak points we can attack. ***As we pretend to pay attention*** we are impatiently waiting for an opening, or internally formulating our rebuttal and planning our devastating comeback that will destroy their argument and make us the victor.

   When I began to learn about listening I discovered that this was my usual mode of listening and The Holy Spirit convicted me of my egotism and pride in always wanting to get my views across. I thank God that I learned this tremendous lesson. People I work with now really believe that I care about their thoughts and concerns and this truth has helped me develop strong relationships and friendships.

2. **Passive** or **Attentive Listening** We live in this mode when we are genuinely interested in hearing and understanding the other person's point of view. We are attentive and passively listen. We

assume that we heard and understand correctly. but stay passive and do not verify it.

Staying in this mode is not productive. It's like being in stagnant water… water that is still and not moving. Stagnant water is a breeding ground for mosquitoes and other pests. We want more from our listening! We want to move onwards to…

3. **Active** or **Reflective Listening** This is the single most useful and most important listening skill. In active listening we are also genuinely interested in understanding what the other person is thinking, feeling, wanting or trying to understand what the message means, and we are active in checking out our understanding before we respond with our own new message. We restate or paraphrase our understanding of their message and reflect it back to the sender for verification. This verification or feedback process is what distinguishes active listening and makes it effective.

This mode of listening is the one that creates strong bonds between the speaker and the hearer. It's exemplified in Solomon's words: "Iron sharpens iron so am man sharpens the countenance of his friend". Your followers will LOVE you when you listen this way. It will revolutionize your life!

Let’s look at 8 barriers to effective listening

Nearly every aspect of human life could be improved by better listening -- from family matters to corporate business affairs to international relations and for us; better Churches.

Most of us are terrible listeners. We are, in fact, such poor listeners that we don't even know how much we're missing! The following are eight common barriers to good listening, with suggestions for overcoming each.

#1 - Knowing the answer

"Knowing the answer" means that you think you already know what the speaker wants to say before they actually finish saying it. You might then impatiently cut her off or try to complete the sentence for her. Even more disruptive is interrupting her by saying that you with disagree her, but without letting her finish saying what it is that you think you disagree with. That's a common problem when a discussion gets heated, and which causes the discussion to degrade quickly.

By interrupting the speaker and not letting her finish, you're essentially saying that you don't value what she's saying. Showing respect to the speaker is a crucial element of good listening.

The "knowing the answer" barrier also causes the listener to prejudge what the speaker is saying – this is a form of closed-mindedness.

A good listener tries to keep an open, receptive mind. He looks for opportunities to stretch his mind when listening, and to acquire new ideas or insights, rather than reinforcing existing points of view.

Strategy for overcoming this barrier

A simple strategy for overcoming the "knowing the answer" barrier is to wait for three seconds after the speaker finishes before beginning your reply.

Three seconds can seem like a very long time during a heated discussion, and following this rule also means that you might have to listen for a long time before the other person finally stops speaking. That's usually a good thing, because it gives the speaker a chance to fully vent his or her feelings.

It's worth emphasizing that the goal of good listening is simply to listen -- nothing more and nothing less.

Using this strategy, most people will probably discover at least one gem -- and often more than one -- no matter whom the conversation is with.

#2 - Trying to be helpful

Another significant barrier to good listening is "trying to be helpful".

Although trying to be helpful may seem beneficial, it interferes with listening because the listener is thinking about how to solve what he perceives to be the speaker's problem. Consequently, he misses what the speaker is actually saying.

An old Zen proverb says, "When walking, walk. When eating, eat." In other words, give your whole attention to whatever you're doing. It's worth emphasizing that the goal of good listening is simply to listen -- nothing more and nothing less. Interrupting the speaker in order to offer advice disrupts the flow of conversation, and impairs the listener's ability to understand the speaker's experience.

Many people have a "messiah complex" and try to fix or rescue other people as a way of feeling fulfilled. Such people usually get a kick out of being problem-solvers, perhaps because it gives them a sense of importance. However, that behavior can be a huge hurdle to good listening.

Trying to be helpful while listening also implies that you've made certain judgments about the speaker. That can raise emotional barriers to communication, as judgments can sometimes mean that the listener doesn't have complete respect for the speaker.

In a sense, giving a person your undivided attention while listening is the purest act of love you can offer. Because human beings are such social animals, simply knowing that another person has listened and understood is empowering. Often that's all a person needs in order to solve the problems on his or her own.

If you as a listener step in and heroically offer your solution, you're implying that you're more capable of seeing the solution than the speaker is. And, if the speaker is describing a difficult or long-term problem, and you offer a facile, off-the-cuff solution, you're probably forgetting that he or she may have already considered your instant solution long before and they may feel like you are trivializing their situation.

Strategy for overcoming this barrier

Schedule a separate session for giving advice. Many people forget that it's rude to offer advice when the speaker isn't asking for it. Even if the advice is good.

In any case, a person can give better advice if he first listens carefully and understands the speaker's complete situation before trying to offer advice. If you believe you have valuable advice that the speaker isn't likely to know, then first politely ask if you may offer what you see as a possible solution. Wait for the speaker to clearly invite you to go ahead before you offer your advice.

#3 - Treating discussion as competition

Some people feel that agreeing with the speaker during a heated discussion is a sign of weakness. They feel compelled to challenge every point the speaker makes, even if they inwardly agree. Discussion then becomes a contest, with a score being kept for who wins the most points by arguing. Treating discussion as competition is one of the most serious barriers to good listening. It greatly inhibits the listener from stretching and seeing a different point of view. It can also be frustrating for the speaker.

Strategy for overcoming this barrier

Although competitive debate serve many useful purposes, and can be great fun, debating should be scheduled for a separate session of its own, where it won't interfere with good listening. Except in a very rare case where you truly disagree with absolutely everything the speaker is saying, you should avoid dismissing their statements completely. Instead, affirm the points of agreement.

Try to voice active agreement whenever you do agree, and be very specific about what you disagree with. A good overall listening principle is to be generous with the speaker. Offer affirmative feedback as often as you feel comfortable doing so. Generosity also entails clearly voicing exactly where you disagree, as well as where you agree.

#4 - Trying to influence or impress

Because good listening depends on listening just for the sake of listening, any ulterior motive will diminish the effectiveness of the listener. Examples of ulterior motives are trying to impress or to influence the speaker. A person who has an agenda other than simply to understand what the speaker is thinking and feeling will not be able to pay complete attention while listening.

Psychologists have pointed out that people can understand language about two or three times faster than they can speak. That implies that a listener has a lot of extra mental "bandwidth" for thinking about other things while listening. A good listener knows how to use that spare capacity to think about what the speaker is talking about. But a listener with an ulterior motive, such as to influence or impress the speaker, will probably use the spare capacity to think about his "next move" in the conversation -- his rebuttal or what he will say next when the speaker is finished -- instead of focusing on understanding the speaker.

Strategy for overcoming this barrier

"Trying to influence or impress" is a difficult barrier to overcome, because motives usually can't just be willed away. Deciding not to have a motive usually only drives it beneath your awareness so that it becomes a hidden motive.

One strategy is to **make note of your internal motives** while you're listening. Simply by noticing your motives, any ulterior motives will eventually unravel, allowing you to let go and to listen just for the sake of listening.

#5 - Reacting to red flag words

Words can provoke a reaction in the listener that wasn't necessarily what the speaker intended. When that happens the listener won't be able to hear or pay full attention to what the speaker is saying. Red flag words or expressions trigger an unexpectedly strong association in the listener's mind, often because of the listener's private beliefs or experiences.

Good listeners have learned how to minimize the distraction caused by red flag words, but a red flag word will make almost any listener momentarily unable to hear with full attention. An important point is that the speaker may not have actually meant the word in the way that the listener understood. However, the listener will be so distracted by the red flag that she will not notice what the speaker actually did mean to say.

Red flag words don't always provoke emotional reactions. Sometimes they just cause slight disagreements or misunderstandings. Whenever a listener finds himself disagreeing or reacting, he should be on the lookout for red flag words.

Strategy for overcoming this barrier

When a speaker uses a word or expression that triggers a reflexive association, you as a good listener can ask the speaker to confirm whether she meant to say what you think she said. When you hear a word or expression that raises a red flag, try to stop the conversation, if possible, so that you don't miss anything that the speaker says. Then ask the speaker to clarify and explain the point in a different way.

#6 - Believing in language

One of the trickiest barriers is "believing in language" -- a misplaced trust in the precision of words. Language is a guessing game. Speaker and listener use language to predict what each other is thinking. Meaning must always be actively negotiated.

It's a fallacy to think that a word's dictionary definition can be transmitted directly through using the word. An example of that fallacy is revealed in the statement, "I said it perfectly clearly, so why didn't you understand?". Of course, the naive assumption here is that words that are clear to one person are clear to another, as if the words themselves contained absolute meaning.

Words have a unique effect in the mind of each person, because each person's experience is unique. Those differences can be small, but the overall effect of the differences can become large enough to cause misunderstanding. A worse problem is that words work by pointing at experiences shared by speaker and listener. If the listener hasn't had the experience that the speaker is using the word to point at, then the word points at nothing. Worse still, the listener may quietly substitute a different experience to match the word.

Strategy for overcoming this barrier

You as a good listener ought to practice mistrusting the meaning of words. Ask the speaker supporting questions to cross-verify what the words mean to him. Don't assume that words or expressions mean exactly the same to you as they do to the speaker. You can stop the speaker and question the meaning of a word. Doing that too often also becomes an impediment, of course, but if you suspect that the speaker's usage of the word might be slightly different, you ought to take time to explore that, before the difference leads to misunderstanding.

#7 - Mixing up the forest and the trees

A common saying refers to an inability "to see the forest for the trees". Sometimes people pay such close attention to detail, that they miss the overall meaning or context of a situation. Some speakers are what we will call "tree" people. They prefer concrete, detailed explanations. They might explain a complex situation just by naming or describing its characteristics in no particular order.

Other speakers are "forest" people. When they have to explain complex situations, they prefer to begin by giving a sweeping, abstract bird's-eye view.

Good explanations usually involve both types, with the big-picture "forest" view providing context and overall meaning, and the specific "trees" view providing illuminating examples. When trying to communicate complex information, the speaker needs to accurately shift between forest and trees in order to show how the details fit into the big picture. However, speakers often forget to signal that they are shifting from one to another, which can cause confusion or misunderstanding for the listener.

Each style is prone to weaknesses in communication. For example, "tree" people often have trouble telling their listener which of the details are more important and how those details fit into the overall context. They can also fail to tell their listener that they are making a transition from one thought to another.

"Forest" people, on the other hand, often baffle their listeners with obscure abstractions. They tend to prefer using concepts, but sometimes those concepts are so removed from the world of the senses that their listeners get lost.

"Tree" people commonly accuse "forest" people of going off on tangents or speaking in unwarranted generalities. "Forest" people commonly feel that "tree" people are too narrow and literal.

Strategy for overcoming this barrier

You as a good listener can explicitly ask the speaker for overall context or for specific exemplary details, as needed. You should cross-verify by asking the speaker how the trees fit together to form the forest. Having an accurate picture of how the details fit together is crucial to understanding the speaker's thoughts.

An important point to remember is that a "tree" speaker may become confused or irritated if you as the listener try to supply missing context, and a "forest" speaker may become impatient or annoyed if you try to supply missing examples. A more effective approach is to encourage the speaker to supply missing context or examples by asking him open-ended questions.

Asking open-ended questions when listening is more effective than asking closed-ended ones.

For example, an open-ended question such as "Can you give me a concrete example of that?" is less likely to cause confusion or disagreement than a more closed-ended one such as "Would such-and-such be an example of what you're talking about?" Some speakers may even fail to notice that a closed-ended question is actually a question. They may then disagree with what they thought was a statement of opinion, and that will cause distracting friction or confusion. The strategy of asking open-ended questions, instead of closed-ended or leading questions, is an important overall component of good listening.

#8 - Over-splitting or over-lumping

People have different styles of organizing thoughts when explaining complex situations. Some people, "splitters", tend to pay more attention to how things are different. Other people, "lumpers", tend to look for how things are alike. Perhaps this is a matter of temperament. If the speaker and listener are on opposite sides of the splitter-lumper spectrum, the different mental styles can cause confusion or lack of understanding.

A listener who is an over-splitter can inadvertently signal that he disagrees with the speaker over everything, even if he actually agrees with most of what the speaker says and only disagrees with a nuance or point of emphasis. That can cause "noise" and interfere with the flow of conversation. Likewise, a listener who is an over-lumper can let crucial differences of opinion go unchallenged, which can lead to a serious misunderstanding later. The speaker will mistakenly assume that the listener has understood and agreed.
It's important to achieve a good balance between splitting (critical thinking) and lumping (metaphorical thinking). Even more important is for the listener to recognize when the speaker is splitting and when she is lumping.

Strategy for overcoming this barrier

An approach to overcoming this barrier when listening is to ask questions to determine more precisely where you agree or disagree with what the speaker is saying, and then to explicitly point that out, when appropriate. For example, you might say, "I think we have differing views on several points here, but do we at least agree that _________?" or "We agree with each other on most of this, but I think we have different views in the area of _________."
By actively voicing the points of convergence and divergence, the listener can create a more accurate mental model of the speaker's mind. That reduces the conversational noise that can arise when speaker and listener fail to realize how their minds are aligned or unaligned.

Good listening is arguably one of the most important skills to have in today's complex world. Families need good listening to face complicated stresses together. Corporate employees need it to solve complex problems quickly and stay competitive. Students need it to understand complex issues in their fields. Ministers need it to be better shepherds of God's Flock. Much can be gained by improving listening skills.

When the question of how to improve communication comes up, most attention is paid to making people better speakers or writers (the "supply side" of the communication chain) rather than on making them better listeners or readers (the "demand side").

To a certain extent, listening is more crucial than speaking

An especially skillful listener will know how to overcome many of the deficiencies of a vague or disorganized speaker. On the other hand, it won't matter how eloquent or cogent a speaker is if the listener isn't paying attention

Chapter Fifteen

Your Master Identity

(One of my favorite chapters FD)

This book is not just about Leadership but it is also about "Finding Your Biblical Style". Hopefully this chapter will help make your style stand out for you to see it clearly. Once that happens you become empowered within yourself.

This is a revelation that I received from the Lord as He began to show me who I was deep inside. As this revelation unfolded before me I could clearly see myself and many of the people in my life. I hope the same thing happens to you as you read this and begin to see into the inner depths of your life. By the end of this chapter when you are assured of your Master Identity you will also have a firm grip on your Purpose. Knowing your Identity empowers you in your Purpose! Then, as you link your Identity, your Purpose and your Biblical Style of Leadership you will definitely be Affirmed in who you are.

Let's l0ok at this example: **John 13:3-5 (NLT)**
"Jesus knew that the Father had given him authority over everything and that he had come from God and would return to God. So he got up from the table, took off his robe, wrapped a towel around his waist, and poured water into a basin. Then he began to wash the disciples' feet, drying them with the towel he had around him."

Jesus knew who He was. He knew where He came from and where He was going… In other words, He knew His Biblical Style of Leadership and then ENABLED Him to wash His Disciples feet. He demonstrated that True Leadership was exemplified in Servanthood.

In this chapter I will introduce you to the "Four Faces" we see in the in several places in the Bible and to help you discover which one you are. Once you see yourself I'm sure you will have a deep desire and the will to shape and develop your Master Identity and be all that God created you to be.

I believe that there are 4 Master Identities and that everyone has one that they make their own during their formative years. And, while everyone has one Master Identity it appears that we all have a mixture of one or two or even all of the others. But always, one will stand out. It is the one that we own deep in our souls. It is crafted and perfected through the circumstances of our early, formative years. It is the one that makes us fit in how and where we want to. And we, being imperfect, fallen human beings, develop it in a selfish way. A way that always has our self at the center.

Here are some Scriptures to help you see how this is revealed through the Word of God.

Revelation 4:6 – 7 "And before the throne there was a sea of glass like unto crystal: and in the midst of the throne, and round about the throne, were four beasts full of eyes before and behind. And the first beast was like a lion, and the second beast like a calf, and the third beast had a face as a man, and the fourth beast was like a flying eagle."

Ezekiel 1:5, 10 "Also out of the midst thereof came the likeness of four living creatures. And this was their appearance; they had the likeness of a man. As for the likeness of their faces, they four had the face of a **man**, and the face of a **lion**, on the right side: and they four had the face of an **ox** on the left side; they four also had the face of an **eagle**."

Ephesians 4:22-24 "Put off, regarding the old way of living, the old man which is corrupt… And be renewed (rebuilt or renovated) in the spirit of your mind (your personality); by putting on the new man, which after God is created in righteousness and true holiness.

It seems to be a truism that people have developed their personality by the time they are between 12 and 14 years of age. How was it developed? Well, as a baby and toddler we find that certain things we do create a reaction in others. We process those reactions and keep the ones that seem to work for us. Then as we get a little older and become teenagers we become very concerned with what other people think about us; especially our peers. So, the ***motivating factor*** in the development of most personalities is fear; the fear of not fitting in and being accepted by those we feel are important. By the time we are between 12 and 14 we have had enough life experiences to create our personality. Therefore, and think about this, the truth is that the blueprint or template for the rest of your life was developed by an immature, defensive, reactionary adolescent who was more concerned with fitting in and not being made fun off than anything else in life!

This is why people are like rivers. Rivers are never strait. They are crooked because they follow the path of least resistance. The path of least resistance is what shaped your personality.

I want to use the Patriarch Jacob as our main example. The name Jacob literally means "DECEIVER". Because of our fallen nature, every man and woman is both a Deceiver and is Self-Deceived. God's answer to this dilemma is to confront us with the truth about who we are. Nowhere is this better shown than in the story of Jacob wrestling with the Angel in Genesis 32:3-28. It is here that he "wrestles with an Angel" all night and in the end is asked, "What is your name?" The Angel knew his name of course, the question is really... "What kind of a man are you?" He replies; "I am Jacob; a deceiver".

He faces his true Master Identity and when he sees himself he humbly accepts who he is and then he has a change in his Heart! God changes his name to prove it. He becomes 'Israel', a Prince who has wrestled with God and 'prevailed'! God wants us all to wrestle with Him and face ourselves.

Very simply, there are 4 Master Identities and we all have one of them or a combination of them where one is dominant. Understand that people try to "CONTROL" others through their Master Identities.

These Master Identities develop within early childhood. Children learn to be like their parents or siblings OR they develop a different Master Identity because of them.

Let's look at the 4 Master Identities

We develop one of these as our own Master Identity in order to be able to have a sense of control in our own lives and to control others. Parents and others who are very close to us in our early years are the influencers that help shape our personality. Basically we make choices to either become like them or to become the opposite of them.

1. **THE INTIMIDATOR**
2. **THE INTERROGATOR**
3. **THE DETACHED PERSON**
4. **THE VICTIM**

Let's see them one at a time…

1. **THE INTIMIDATOR:** This person is ***Aggressive*** and ***Threatening***

   This person will uses threats or force to get their way

   This person loves to push people around

2. **THE INTERROGATOR**: This person has a ***Superior Attitude***

   They will ask questions or question the actions of another to find a way to belittle them.

   As the other person grows smaller, the Interrogator grows bigger.

   This person loves to put people down with their words.

3. **THE DETACHED:** This person always appears ***Apathetic*** and ***Aloof***

   They don't get involved and so they cannot get hurt.

   They just don't seem to care.

   This person loves to drop out and bury their feelings

   They thrive on the attention they get but give none back.

4. **THE VICTIM**: This is the one with the ***Poor Me Attitude***

   This person loves to feel sorry for themselves and is always making other people feel sorry for them too.

   They act as "martyrs".

   They are always asking "Why me?"

In order for us to be TRANSFORMED into the person God

wants you to be you have to wrestle with God like Jacob did! God is not going to make these changes for us. He expects us to cooperate with Him. He has already done the work inside of us when we accepted Jesus Christ as our Savior. We ARE new creations in Christ.

This is where we see the Scripture come alive:

Philippians 2:12 "Wherefore, my beloved, as ye have always obeyed, not as in my presence only, but now much more in my absence, ***work out your own salvation*** with fear and trembling."

The truth is that we created our personality and now God wants us to "re-create" it!

Does that seem strange?
Can we really recreate our personalities? Absolutely!

Let's re-read Ephesians 4:22-24

"Put off, regarding the old way of living, the old man which is corrupt… And be renewed (rebuilt or renovated) in the spirit of your mind (your personality); by putting on the new man, which after God is created in righteousness and true holiness.

We have to consciously decide to "***put off the old man***" and "***put on the new***".

So, like Jacob, you must wrestle with God to be transformed! That's how you will recognize your Master Identity and start the process of transformation.

Two things that happened to Jacob

1. God changed his name to Israel signifying a Character or Personality Change
2. He walked with a limp for the rest of his life to remind him of who he used to be and who he had now become.

Remember, many are called but few are chosen…
If you want to be transformed you have to work at it!

And also remember that in order for you to become what God wants us to become He will orchestrate things in our lives placing you us the exact circumstances we need to be in giving us opportunities to change…

Once you see your Master Identity you will immediately recognize the transformation that is to take place as you see yourself in the Faces of the Lion, the Eagle, The Man or the Ox.

First the Intimidator… This is the Face of the Lion

The INTIMIDATOR becomes a SERVANT

The Intimidator used to use their strength to abuse people with threats and violence

The Lion uses its strength to bless and protect people

Second, the Interrogator… This is the Face of the Eagle

The INTERROGATOR becomes HUMBLE

The Interrogator used their words to put people down

The Eagle uses their words to lift people up

The Eagle lifts them up to the high places showing them that they can get oil and honey out of the rock.

Jesus said; "He who would be greatest, let him be the least among you."

Third, the Detached Person… This is the Face of the Ox

The DETACHED PERSON becomes a CARING PERSON

The Ox is finds it strength and purpose as it is yoked to another.

The Ox attaches itself to other people getting involved in people's lives and no longer lives a detached, uncaring life.

As the Ox matures they start to Mentor others just like Jesus did.

"Take my yoke upon you and learn of me"

Fourth, the Victim…This is the Face of A REAL MAN

The VICTIM becomes a GRATEFUL PERSON

The Grateful Person strives to become like Christ who willingly laid down his life for others.

They say: "Don't weep or feel sorry for me…"

The Grateful Person presents their body to God "as a living sacrifice"

Now, you are a true martyr; one of Jesus' witnesses (Greek: martyrs)

So, how we do we begin the process of Transformation?

There are 3 things you MUST begin to do NOW to be *TRANSFORMED*

1. Look into yourself and **IDENTIFY YOUR MASTER IDENTITY** and then **HONESTLY** confront yourself
2. Look at the **OPPOSING FACE** that I've shown you in this chapter and recognize that what kind of a person **YOU ARE DESTINED TO BECOME.**
3. **CONSCIOUSLY CONFRONT YOURSELF** each day and "**PUT OFF THE OLD**" and ask the Lord how to "**PUT ON THE NEW**".

If you do this for 21 days you will see TRANSFORMATION begin to take place!

So which face is yours???

Who will you become???

Do you see that each face is the face of Jesus???

Chapter Sixteen

Things to Think About

2 Timothy 2:2 says: "And the things that thou hast heard of me among many witnesses, the same **commit thou to faithful men**, who shall be able to teach others also."

Jesus, the greatest leader of all focused on his 12. Everything and everyone else was on the periphery.

Leaders live in two "time zones". Leadership helps us to walk in the present and the future at the same time.

Leadership is getting people to do what you want them to do in such a manner that makes them feel like they are doing what they want to do without feeling coerced to do it.

A prince who wanted to thank Arnold Palmer gave him the title to a Country Club because Arnold said that he collected "golf clubs" literally meaning an iron or a wood but the Prince did not think on that level so he bought him a "Golf Club"! He couldn't think on that low level. He thought on a higher level. We have to get our people to think on a higher level too.

We have to think about our motives for leadership… Are they power, prestige, etc. or are they discipleship and multiplication.

As you grow through this process of Finding Your Biblical Style of Leadership you are going to find that your hindsight is going to become someone else's foresight and you will have successfully led them to look towards their own future.

Purpose in Ministry

Here are the Fivefold Ministries as seen as One Man

Apostle –	The Father's Heart revealing compassion and strategies for Advancing the Kingdom
Prophet –	The Mouth communicating guidance
Teacher –	The Mind of Christ bringing wisdom and understanding
Pastor –	The Feet leading the sheep to pasture
Evangelist –	The Hands reaching out to souls

Designing Your Life

When we begin to look at our lives with the intention of "Designing" it there are some questions that you must ask yourself…

1. What are some of the dreams that you have had?
2. What are some of the promises that you have made to yourself?
3. You need to ask yourself what do you want to "be"?

4. Then you have to ask yourself what do you want to "do"?
5. Then ask yourself what do you want to "have"?

Make a list of these things and then "milestone" them at about 1 year out.

Some examples would be:

- Write a book
- Write a song
- Go to college
- Go to night school
- Change your career

At the appointed milestone time ask yourself

1. Have you started?
2. Have you accomplished anything?
3. Do you need to allot more time to this?

Chapter Seventeen
Mission & Vision Statements

To succeed as a Leader you need to develop a Mission and a Vision Statement.

You can start here and practice writing a Mission Statement along with a Vision Statement…

A Mission Statement is a declaration of what you are here to do and accomplish.

It can be either one or just a few sentences and easily memorized and communicated to others.

The understanding you have of your Mission will develop over time… so, just write it as you see it today. Once a Mission Statement is finalized it will probably be ready for editing within 3 to 5 years.

A Vision Statement explains how you are going to accomplish your Mission.

You will probably have several steps to accomplish as you work towards accomplishing your Mission.

Here is part of an interview you can read. It's with Laurie Beth

Jones, author of THE PATH

What's the best way to form a sense of mission?

Following are the three elements of a good mission statement:

A mission statement should be no longer than a single sentence. People who accomplish a lot with their lives have laser-like focus. This focus enables them to zero in on what their mission is and state it succinctly. One of the most powerful mission statements in history was given to a 14-year-old French girl. She received a message that, essentially, was:

Dear Joan,

Save France!

Love,

God

That girl was, of course, Joan of Arc, and with no resources other than her faith, she rallied the French army and won battle after battle. And it was all because of that two-word mission statement: Save France.

Your mission statement should be so concise and simple that an average 12-year-old would hear it and then say, "Oh, I get it. This is what you do."

You should be able to recite your mission statement from memory. This means your mission needs to constantly be in your heart. You face decisions every day that are going to either take you closer to where you want to be or take you farther away.

Webster's Dictionary defines "mission" as a clearly defined territory of responsibility that is assigned by a higher headquarters as part of a larger plan. A mission is felt as a calling. I believe everyone is given a divine mission, and it's our job to find out what it is -- and then do it.

We often feel like we have to do it all; that we're responsible for everything. Once you get clear about your mission you'll sleep easier at night because you'll know how to choose your battles.

What are some of the myths about mission?

One myth is "My job is my mission." A mission is not a job description; it's always larger than your job description. For example, let's say you ask someone about their mission in life, and they say, "To be a doctor." What that person has given you is a job description; their actual mission is probably healing. The truth is, if your mission is healing there are many ways to heal. Your job is a temporary means of delivering your mission.

Women seem to have gotten trapped in another myth: "My role is my mission." Many times if you ask a woman what her mission in life is, she'll say, "To be a good wife and mother." Who was she before she got married? Who is she going to be when the kids are grown? Women can get very tied up in their roles. They need to be aware that their roles can change. Your mission is larger than your role.

Some people think their mission is their "to-do" list. To-do lists should only be developed after you've written down your mission and your vision statement. A vision statement is a long, flowery description of what the landscape will look like as you accomplish your mission. The Founding Fathers got together and said, "We are here in order to form a more perfect union." That was their mission statement. Then somebody said, "What would a more perfect union look like?" And that's when they had to define it with the Bill of Rights. (In a more perfect union, we would have freedom of speech; we would have freedom of religion….) The Bill of Rights is the vision of this country.

People always buy into visions, either their own or someone else's. We all absolutely have to have a vision. "Where there is no vision, people perish." Don't write your to-do list until you know your mission and your vision. Stephen Covey says that people get caught up doing urgent things that are not important. Once you are working from your vision, you are doing the important things that may not have seemed so urgent before you got it clear.

Three steps to success

1. **Get specific goals**

Joan of Arc's mission was to save France. Her vision was to get the Dauphin crowned. Her first goal was to get off the farm; then get a horse; then ride to the Dauphin; then get permission to talk to the generals of the army. That's getting specific about what it is you're going to do.

2. **Examine and enlist your resources**

All the men who signed the Declaration of Independence pledged their lives, their fortunes and their sacred honor. They knew they needed an army so they sold land to buy ammunition for the army. Look at what you have; then decide what you can do to get what you need.

3. **Break ranks and be bold**

So many people are marching in place, waiting for someone to give them permission to do something. Leaders give themselves permission.

A mission statement should be a clear and succinct representation of a person's purpose in life. Like a business, it should incorporate socially meaningful and measurable criteria addressing concepts such as the moral/ethical position of the enterprise, public image, the target market, products/services, the geographic domain and expectations of growth and profitability.

The intent of the Mission Statement should be the first consideration for anyone who is making a strategic decision. The statement can range from a very simple to a very complex set of ideas.

Mission Statements of Well Known Enterprises

The following are some examples of mission statements from real enterprises.

3M	"To solve unsolved problems innovatively"
Mary Kay	"To give unlimited opportunity to women."
Merck	"To preserve and improve human life."
Wal-Mart	"To give ordinary folk the chance to buy the same thing as rich people."
Walt Disney	"To make people happy."

These are the 'one-liners', but each is supported by a set of values that set the performance standards and direct the implementation of the mission.

So, when you are preparing your Mission Statement remember to make it clear and succinct, incorporating socially meaningful and measurable criteria and consider approaching it from a grand scale.

In conclusion, I think you can see that Leadership has many facets. Now that you have identified your Master Identity you can develop your Biblical Leadership Style by "putting off the old" and "putting on the new" and experience the joy of having a solid sense of self-worth and an appreciation of what God has placed inside of you.

ABOUT THE AUTHOR

Frank Duprée was raised in Long Island, NY and was Saved in 1969. In 1979, after being in Ministry for several years, along with his wife Giovanna, he came to New Jersey to start Living Water Church in North Arlington. He was Commissioned and Consecrated as an Apostle and Bishop by the late Dr. Wade E. Taylor, Founder of Pinecrest Bible Training Center.

In January of 2000 he founded Metro Apostolic Network, a fellowship that brings Fivefold Gift Ministers together with Marketplace Ministers and Mature Intercessors. The Network is based in Metro New Jersey and has Apostolic Centers in Brooklyn, NY and Atlanta, GA as well as in Kenya and Pakistan.

Apostle Duprée is a Charter Member of The International Coalition of Apostolic Leaders and in 2015 when the US Coalition of Apostolic Leaders was formed out of ICAL he was appointed as the Senior Administrator working alongside of his close friend and USCAL Convener; Apostle Joseph Mattera.

Apostle Duprée also serves on several other Apostolic Councils based in the NY/NJ Metro area. He works closely with Apostle Bernard Wilks of Newark, NJ, and is a Member of the Executive Council of Transformation Newark and is a Founding Member of The Newark Area Apostolic Council.

You can find out more about Apostle Duprée by visiting his website: www.FrankDupree.com There you will also find numerous teachings and videos. You can also sign up for his monthly e-Newsletter there.

46586425R00065

Made in the USA
Middletown, DE
04 August 2017